3,89

J Series Who

Who Was
Albert
Einstein?

Who Was
Albert
Einstein?

by Jess M. Brallier

illustrated by Robert Andrew Parker

Grosset & Dunlap • New York

Text copyright © 2002 by Jess M. Brallier. Illustrations copyright © 2002 by Robert Andrew Parker. Cover illustration copyright © 2002 by Nancy Harrison. All rights reserved. Published by Grosset & Dunlap, a division of Penguin Putnam Books for Young Readers, 345 Hudson Street, New York, NY 10014. GROSSET & DUNLAP is a trademark of Penguin Putnam, Inc. Published simultaneously in Canada. Printed in the U.S.A.

Library of Congress Cataloging-in-Publication Data is available.

ISBN 0-448-42496-7 (pbk)   A B C D E F G H I J
ISBN 0-448-42659-5 (GB)   A B C D E F G H I J

Contents

Who Was
Albert Einstein?

"For an idea that does not at first seem insane, there is no hope."

—Albert Einstein

Did you know that Albert Einstein was a very poor student who got kicked out of school? Well, he was. Yet he was one of the most brilliant people that the world has ever known.

Did you know that Albert was a peace-loving person who hated war? Well, he was. Yet his work led to the creation of the most destructive bomb ever.

Did you know that Albert was shy and hated publicity and attention? Yet he was a media superstar. Even now, fifty years after his death, Hollywood still makes movies about him—and T-shirts, coffee mugs, and posters are decorated with pictures of his famous face.

Who was Albert Einstein? You are about to find out.

Chapter 1
Born to Think

"There are only two ways to live your life. One is as though nothing is a miracle. The other is as though everything is a miracle."

—Albert Einstein

Albert Einstein made his entrance into the world on March 14, 1879, in Ulm, Germany. He certainly didn't seem like an extraordinary child. He was chubby and pale with thick, black hair. He was so quiet and shy that his parents worried that there was something wrong with him. They took Albert to doctors. "He doesn't talk," his parents explained. The doctors found nothing wrong.

The story goes that Albert didn't speak a word until he was three or four years old. Then suddenly, over supper one night, he said, "The soup is too hot." Greatly relieved, his parents asked why he had never said anything before. "Because," little Albert replied, "up to now, everything has been fine." Is this story true? There's no proof.

Most boys his age played soldier and other rough-and-tumble games. Not Albert. When Albert saw real soldiers marching with their blank faces, they frightened him. Albert preferred to stay by himself and day-dream. He enjoyed playing with blocks and building houses out of playing cards—some of them were fourteen stories high.

His parents continued to worry about their lonely and quiet son. They took him to more doctors. "Could there be something wrong with his brain?" his parents asked. Once again, doctors found nothing

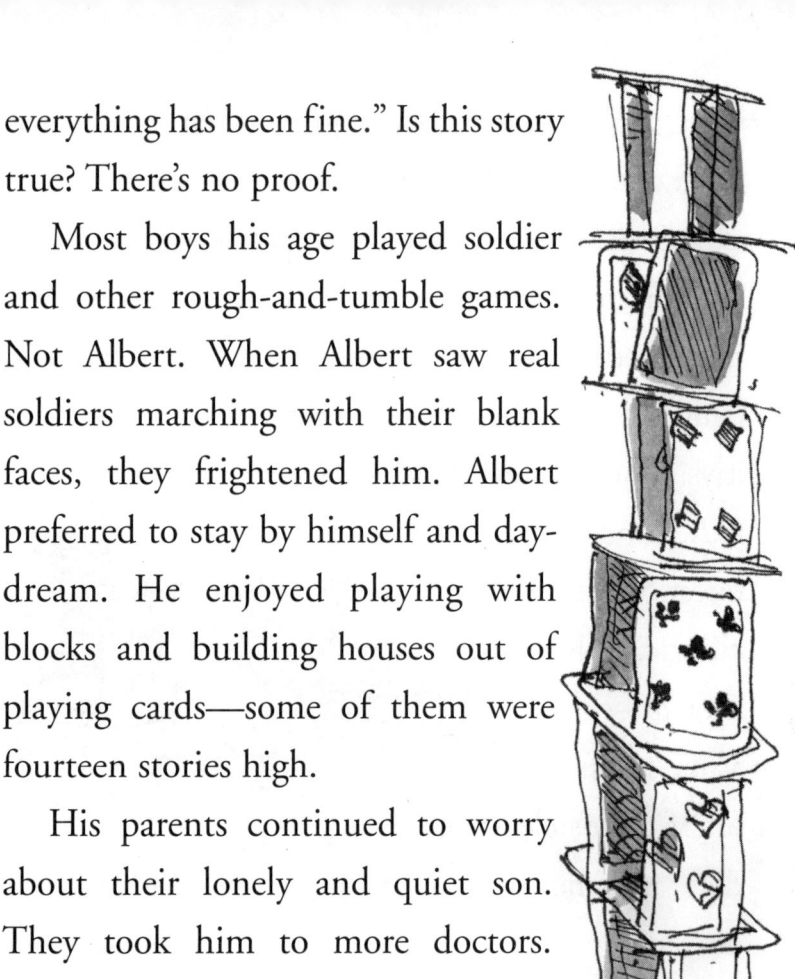

wrong with the boy. It was just his nature. He was quiet. He was a thinker.

Albert's father and uncle had a business that sold batteries, generators, and wire. Electricity fascinated Albert. It was invisible, powerful, and dangerous. Electricity was like some mysterious secret. Albert pestered his father and uncle with lots of questions. How fast is electricity? Is there a way to see it? What's it made of? If there's electricity, could there be other strange and mysterious forces in the universe?

Albert enjoyed thinking about a world beyond the one that could be seen or explained. As he later said, "Imagination is more important than knowledge. Knowledge is limited. Imagination encircles the world."

Albert was also fascinated by the compass that his father had given him. No matter what he did with the compass, its needle always pointed in the same direction: North. Albert turned the compass upside down and sideways. He used it in the dark. No matter what, that needle always pointed in the same direction. Albert wondered why. His dad explained that the earth is like a big magnet that's always pulling on the compass's magnetic needle. Albert was amazed that some strange and powerful force was all around him. He could not see it or feel it. Yet it was there, making the compass needle move.

Albert had more to think about. School wasn't teaching him about the things that mattered to him. So at about age 10, Albert started to teach himself. He was going to read as much about science as he could.

The Magnetic Earth

Magnets have invisible forces. Every magnet has two ends—one called the "north pole" and one called the "south pole." The north pole of any magnet is attracted to the south pole of any other magnet. Bring opposite poles close to each other and they stick together. But try to bring two like poles together—north and north, or south and south—you can't!

The iron inside the earth creates magnetic forces. The earth itself has a north pole end (near the North Pole) and a south pole end (near the South Pole). A compass's needle is magnetic. One end is attracted to the earth's north pole and one to the earth's south pole. There is an arrow on the end of the compass needle that always points north.

Albert also enjoyed playing the violin. Music calmed his active mind. He especially liked playing duets with his mother. She would accompany him on the piano. One day, while they were playing, Albert suddenly realized that music chords were like patterns of numbers. Musical rhythms were like counting by threes, fours, or eights. "Music's just like numbers," he exclaimed to his mother. (Albert was thinking even when relaxing.) Later, when Albert was famous and traveled all around the world, he carried only two things with him—his suitcase and his violin.

When Albert was a year old, his family moved to the city of Munich in Germany. There, his sister, Maja, was born. Albert expected a little sister to be

like a toy. But Maja had no wheels like his other toys. "Where are its wheels?" he asked his parents, clearly disappointed with the new baby.

The wheel-less little girl, however, quickly became Albert's best friend. As they grew older, Albert and Maja loved to take long walks and hikes. Often their cousins came with them. The higher the hill, the better Albert could think. On these thinking hikes, he used his compass and thought more about how mysterious the world

was. He would lie on his back in the grass, look at the sky, and think about space. Is anything farther away than space? How fast would somebody have to go to get there? How does light get all the way from those stars to your eyes? How far does space go on? Could you ride on a beam of light? Is anything bigger than the universe?

It was as if Albert had been born to think. His father and uncles helped guide his thinking. His sister and cousins encouraged his thinking hikes. Albert found books to help him think out math and science problems. And his mother introduced him to music, which engaged his mind in a way that books could not. Just as some kids dream of becoming mechanics or veterinarians, Albert was destined to be a thinker.

Chapter 2
What's to be Done with a Genius?

Albert liked elementary school. The teachers were kind and patient. They tried their best to answer all of Albert's questions. But things changed when Albert turned ten. That's when he started high school. It was an awful experience.

Once, when Albert's father asked the school principal what profession his son should consider, the principal said, "It doesn't matter. Albert will never make a success of himself at anything." The German high

school was very strict. The students had to wear uniforms. They had to march like soldiers from one class to the next. And soldiers made Albert nervous. In the classrooms, everyone had to sit very straight at all times. Teachers yelled out orders. Students jumped to attention. Questions were not allowed. Albert was expected to read and memorize. He was not expected to think. Albert was stunned. This wasn't his style. Albert called his teachers "sergeants" because of how they treated the students.

Math was his favorite subject because you couldn't just memorize math problems—you had to think them through. At home, his uncle made up difficult algebra problems for Albert. Algebra is math that involves equations, and for Albert, it was like solving a puzzle. Albert was also given a book that he used to teach himself geometry. Geometry is math that involves shapes—squares, cubes, circles, and spheres—and for Albert it was like playing with blocks. Meanwhile, other boys in his class were still struggling with multiplying and dividing, and Albert was being punished for asking too many questions.

Albert never really fit
in with the other boys at
school. He wasn't interested
in sports, and the classes
were boring.

Albert needed an older brother —someone who had lived through a rough high school experience— to let him know that everything would turn out okay. For Albert, that "older brother" was Max Talmey. Max was a medical student and a friend of the family. He often joined the Einsteins for dinner. Max quickly came to understand and appreciate how brilliant the teenage Albert was. He brought Albert lots of books from the local university.

Max couldn't really discuss math with Albert. "The flight of Albert's mathematical genius," wrote Max, "was so high that I could no longer follow." But Max did encourage Albert to explore new interests. Soon Albert was reading about history and studying religion.

Albert's family was Jewish. But his parents did not follow many Jewish customs. They had sent Albert to a Roman Catholic elementary school simply because they thought it was the best school available. But for a while, Albert wanted to follow the traditions of the Jewish religion very strictly. For example, he refused to eat pork. Like many people, Albert did not believe the exact words of the Bible, such as passages that said the world had been created in just six days. Did this end Albert's interest in religion? No. It just gave Albert's curious mind even more to think about. "Ideas come from God," he claimed. And later in life, Albert often said that his goal as a scientist was to "read God's mind."

When Albert was fifteen, his friend Max moved to America. Losing Max was very hard on Albert. Then Albert's family moved from Germany to Italy because of his father's business, leaving Albert behind to finish school. Albert was

angry and lonely and hated school more than ever.

Albert had never looked up to his teachers. Now he grew openly disrespectful of them. "Unthinking respect for authority," he explained, "is the greatest enemy of the truth." One of his teachers called him "a lazy dog." Others said that he was a bad influence on his classmates because he was always asking questions the teachers could not answer. The end result was that Albert was expelled from school.

Chapter 3
Albert Takes a Very Deep Breath . . .
and Keeps Thinking

"One is born into a herd of buffaloes and must be glad if one is not trampled underfoot before one's time."

—Albert Einstein

Getting expelled from school—even a school he hated—was very painful for Albert. He was embarrassed to have failed so openly. He was angry with his teachers. He was disappointed in himself. Yet he was also excited that he would soon see his family.

Albert joined his parents and sister in northern Italy. Italy was so different from Germany. Albert quickly fell in love with the country. Italians were so friendly, civilized, and open-minded. For the

next two years, Albert went to
concerts and visited art museums.
Best of all, he had time to read
and to think. He studied the
lives of scientists, including

those who had suffered because their thinking had gone against widely held ideas of the time. For example, there was Nicholas Copernicus (1473–1543), the Polish astronomer. He was severely criticized for stating that the earth orbited around the sun and not vice versa. A hundred years later, in 1633, Galileo Galilei, an Italian scientist, was arrested for agreeing with Copernicus. Yet in Albert's time, no sane person believed that the sun circles the earth.

The study of other scientists' theories pushed Albert's thinking even further. In Italy, he had the time to write down those thoughts and answer many of the questions he had been asking himself for years. Now he was a real scientist. He even had his first scientific paper published in a magazine, while he was still a teenager!

When scientists have new ideas to share, they write about them in scientific journals. (That's what it means to "get a paper published.") For

Albert, as for all scientists,
getting papers published
was very important; it was
the only way other scientists
could learn about his ideas
and thoughts.

Albert's first published paper was about electricity and magnetism. That was no surprise. After all, he'd been thinking about both subjects for years. But to everybody's surprise, Albert began his paper by disagreeing with something that all scientists assumed was true. Scientists claimed that the "empty" part of outer space—the part without planets and moons—was filled with something called "ether." Scientists had no idea what ether was made of, or what it looked like, felt like, or smelled like. But they all agreed it was there. Albert disagreed. He claimed that the empty part of space was, well, empty.

Albert's first paper did not get a lot of attention. Although Albert was disappointed about that, he should not have been surprised. After all, Albert was a teenager who had been expelled from high school and who was still living with his parents. Who was he to challenge the theories of the world's most respected scientists? However, years later, many of those same scientists would seek out Einstein's first published paper and marvel at the genius of the young scientist. Because Albert was right.

While living in Italy, Albert took long walks by himself. Day after day he hiked in the mountains. His family's business was failing, and Albert worried that he was a drain on his parents—a sponge that took but never gave back. He had lots to think about, and a daily walk and time alone cleared his mind. "I lived in solitude in the country and noticed how the monotony of a quiet life stimulates the creative mind," he said.

Albert made several important decisions during those hikes. He decided to study physics at college. Physics is the science of objects, their energy, and the way they move. After that he wanted to become a physics professor. To do this, Albert knew that he would have to finish high school. But no school could ever own his mind, which he felt his German high school had tried to do.

Albert also decided that the freedom to think, to explore his own ideas, would always be the most important thing in life. If he got married and had children, his wife and family would matter to him,

of course. But they would never matter as much, he realized, as his ability to think freely. To some people, that might sound like a selfish way to live.

But for Albert, it was the only kind of life that made any sense.

Albert re-entered high school in Switzerland, where German was spoken. What a pleasant and unexpected surprise! His new school wasn't like the German high school at all. At the Swiss school, students were supposed to ask questions. Albert especially enjoyed discussing the subject of "time" with his teachers. How fast does time pass? What is the future—do we travel into it or is it already here? Will time ever run out?

Not only did Albert like his Swiss school, he also liked the Swiss people. They were friendly and fair. Albert decided to become a citizen of Switzerland. After graduating from high school, Albert stayed in Switzerland and began college at Swiss Federal Polytechnic in the city of Zurich. Albert had no money. His family had fallen on hard times. An uncle provided Albert with a little money. But it wasn't much. Albert lived in a dark room, ate barely enough, and went without new clothes just so he could stay in school.

Still, there were good things about this time. At college he was making new friends. (The other students lovingly would call Albert the "professor" because he had so many theories and talked so much about physics.) One of his new friends was Mileva Maric, the only woman in Albert's class. Albert liked to call her "Dolly." She, too, was a brilliant thinker. They talked endlessly about physics and music. It was not long before Mileva and Albert announced their plans to marry.

("Without the thought of you," he wrote her in 1900 at the age of twenty-one, "I would no longer want to live among this sorry herd of humans.")

Upon graduation from college in 1900, Albert was all set to become a physics teacher. It should have been a wonderful time in his life. He had his diploma, and he was in love. However, he could not find a teaching job. His uncle stopped sending him money. Albert's clothes were ragged. His meals were few and far between. His health suffered. Without a job, he couldn't afford to marry Mileva. Albert ended up taking a job with the Swiss Patent Office. It wasn't where he wanted to work, but it was a job.

Then Albert's father died. Albert was devastated. Fortunately, he had Mileva. And, surprisingly, his job at the patent office turned out to be far better than Albert could have ever imagined.

Chapter 4
The Best Years

When a person invents something—for example, a battery-powered back-scratcher for miniature poodles—the inventor sends a description of the invention to a patent office. An examiner looks at the idea and decides if it's really something new, or just something that is a little bit different from an already-invented gadget. If it's really a new idea, the inventor gets a patent, which means other people aren't allowed to copy it.

It takes a very smart person to understand inventions when they're just at the idea stage. Albert was that person. Reading applications for new inventions was like solving puzzles. Albert was so good at his job that each day he completed his work long before it was time to go home. He then was able to turn his attention to his first love—thinking. Imagine what this must have been like for Albert. It would be like a kid going to school every morning, finishing all the schoolwork within an hour, and then playing for the rest of the day.

With all that time to think, Albert ended up writing and publishing more scientific papers. In one year alone, he published five groundbreaking papers in a very famous German journal about physics. "A storm broke loose in my mind," explained Albert. So in some ways, his patent office job turned out to be a lot better than the teaching job that he had originally hoped for.

Einstein in 4-D

People measure objects in three ways: length, width, and depth. Anything—a piece of toast, a TV, a yo-yo—is so many inches high, so many inches wide, and so many inches thick. These three ways of measuring are known as dimensions.

Albert threw in a fourth dimension—time.

Albert said that the dimension of time was as important as length, width, and depth—especially when measuring something really big like outer space. To think about the size of outer space but not the time it takes for something to travel through that space is like thinking about a song without the lyrics. Something important is missing.

With steady work at the patent office, Albert felt that he could ask Mileva to marry him. So he did. She said "yes," and they were married in 1903. The following year, their son, Hans Albert, was born. Now Albert had the time to enjoy music, long dinners, and long walks with his family.

Albert was happy and secure. Confident in his job, he could relax—be more himself. For Albert, that meant dressing carelessly, wearing the same wrinkled shirt day after day, and often forgetting to brush his hair. As someone once said, "Einstein looked as if he'd just smoked an exploding cigar."

Albert's years at the patent office were wonderful. He had a family, time to think and write lots of scientific papers, and enough money. Many of the greatest scientific achievements of the twentieth century—electronics, the atomic bomb, space travel—were all suggested by Einstein in the papers he published while he worked at the patent office. Those ideas were then worked on further by other scientists in the decades that followed.

Then in 1909, the University of Zurich convinced Albert to leave the patent office and become a professor. Albert would actually be paid to teach and study physics. Life was even more wonderful.

Einstein's Theory of *Relativity*

In 1905, Albert published a paper about "relativity." It said that everything—except light—travels at different speeds depending upon different situations.

Think about relativity this way:

If you look up at the sky and see a plane in the distance, it doesn't appear as if it is going very fast. You stand there and watch as the plane seems to move slowly across the sky.

Yet if you were standing next to it, the plane would zoom past you in a split second. BLAM! BOOM! Gone!

And yet again, if you're sitting inside the plane, it barely seems to move at all.

See how the speed of that one plane can look totally different to you in different situations? That was Albert's point. The speed of a moving object depends on how it's being viewed.

In a short time, Albert became a very popular professor. College students enjoyed the way he explained difficult concepts with simple images. (Think about this image: "A man falling freely in the earth's gravitational field who drops an object will not notice it is falling.") And Albert loved to lecture: "It is the supreme art of the teacher to awaken joy in creative expression and knowledge." Albert was invited to speak all over Europe. He was a rising star. Albert accepted other teaching jobs that took him not only to Zurich but to other European cities, like Bern, Prague, and Munich.

An Einstein Thought

Before Einstein, scientists thought that the sun was always in the same place, with the Earth and other planets orbiting around it. Think of the sun and planets as being like your neighborhood. Your home is always on the same street. Your school stays in one spot. You don't have to go looking for these places every morning.

Albert, however, shocked everybody by claiming that the sun, the other stars, the planets—everything, all of the time—are moving through space. Think of a parade, with bands and floats always staying the same distance from each other. But the whole parade is moving down the street.

Albert's theories were startling. For example, Albert claimed that light bent as it traveled through space. This surprised scientists who assumed that light always traveled in a straight line. Who was right? Often a scientific theory can't be proven. But this theory could be. During a total solar eclipse, the moon blocks the sun's bright light from viewers on Earth. This makes it possible to photograph the light of the stars beyond the sun. Albert insisted that a study of those photos would show light bending as it passed other planets and the sun.

All Albert needed to do was wait about four years for the next total eclipse, in 1914. Many scientists were also excited to see whether Albert's light theory was correct. In 1911, plans were begun to send a group of scientists to

Russia to test Albert's theory. Russia was one of the best locations from which to photograph the stars during the eclipse.

Of course, 1914 was still far in the future. In the meantime, Albert continued to think, give lectures, and develop his "eccentric genius" style. Hopelessly absentminded, he often forgot his apartment key (even on his wedding night), lost luggage, forgot to eat, and used money as a bookmark (then lost the book). He always buttoned just the top button of his coats. Why? "It's simpler that way," he said. When Albert shaved, he used only water—which is a very painful way to shave. So a friend gave him shaving cream. Albert tried it, said it was marvelous, and then went back to using water. Why was that? "It's simpler that way," he replied.

Questioned about his odd look, he explained, "It would be a sad situation if the wrapper were better than the meat wrapped inside it." What was really amazing was how Albert was becoming popular with people who had no interest in science. With his wild hair, mismatched socks, wrinkled shirts, and pants that were too short, Albert was not just a brilliant physics professor. He was a personality. His mysterious smile beamed from the front pages of newspapers around the world—a genius who had unlocked the secrets of God's own mind. People who didn't understand a bit of his physics, who didn't know an isobar from an ice cream bar, were fascinated by Albert Einstein. Articles about Albert showed up in many magazines and newspapers. Had TV already been invented, Albert would have been the subject of all kinds of hour-long specials.

Famous Formula
Warning! Hard Stuff!

$E = mc^2$ is a scientific formula. It is so short that it looks simple, not much harder than $2 + 2 = 4$.

That's part of the reason this formula is so brilliant. Albert figured out that a very difficult concept could be explained in a very brief way. ("Make things as simple as possible but not simpler.")

"E" stands for *energy*, and "m" is for *mass*. Mass is the amount of matter in something. Mass is a little bit like weight. The third thing, "c" is for the *speed of light*. Light travels really, really fast. (Ever try to outrun it?)

Basically, what the formula says is that when a little bit of mass is changed into energy, a whole lot of energy will be released.

That's what happens with an atomic bomb. An atom is split; mass changes to energy; and an incredible amount of destructive energy is released.

With this formula, Einstein claimed that all matter, from a feather to a rock, contains energy.

Chapter 5
Albert Hits High Gear

"If A equals success, then the formula is A equals X plus Y plus Z. X is work. Y is play. Z is keeping your mouth shut."

—Albert Einstein

In 1913, a famous university offered to pay Albert more money than he had ever made before. And all he had to do was come to the school and think. He would teach only when he felt like it. It was a dream come true . . . almost. The one drawback was that the university was in Berlin, Germany.

BERLIN

GERMANY

SWITZERLAND

Although it had been nearly twenty years since Albert last lived in Germany, he hadn't forgotten his awful high school years. And Albert's wife, Mileva, didn't like Berlin or the people there. She thought they were mean and unfriendly.

Mileva was also jealous of Albert's success. She was a brilliant scientist. But the world only cared about Albert. The more she thought about it, the less she wanted to leave Zurich and their many friends.

Albert had to make a decision: Would he go off to Berlin to think, or stay in Zurich and be a good husband and father? Albert needed brilliant people around him who could help him think about his ideas. At the time, a scientist said, "Only a dozen men in the world understand relativity, and eight of them live in Berlin." Albert remembered his hikes through Italy and the promises he had made to himself. He decided to go to Berlin.

Albert left Mileva and their two children

behind in Switzerland. Albert once admitted, "I treat my wife as an employee whom one cannot fire." It was not surprising that Mileva and Albert soon got divorced. Thereafter, Albert had little to do with her or their two sons. Years later, when Albert won the Nobel Prize in 1922, he sent the prize money to Mileva and their sons. Perhaps this made him feel less guilty for having abandoned his family.

Albert's oldest son, Hans Albert, grew up to become a distinguished science professor in California. Occasionally he visited with his father. Eduard, born in 1910, the younger son—whom Albert nicknamed "Tedel," which means "little bear"—was gifted in music and literature but suffered from mental illness. After his mother's death, Eduard lived in a hospital for the rest of his life.

Albert once congratulated his son Hans Albert—whose birthday he never remembered—for being just like himself when it came to family.

"It is a joy for me to have a son who has inherited the main trait of my personality: the ability to rise above mere existence by sacrificing oneself through the years for an impersonal goal. This is the best, indeed the only way in which we can make ourselves independent from personal fate and from other human beings." Albert never questioned his decision to choose scientific discovery over family.

Albert and the Tube

In 1922, Albert won a Nobel Prize—the most important award a scientist can ever win—for the thinking he did about "the photoelectrical effect." Albert's thinking about the photoelectrical effect then led to the invention of TV. (You can thank Albert for the boob tube.)

As for moving to Berlin, Mileva had good reason for not wanting to live in Germany. In the early 1900s, the countries of Europe were struggling with each other for power. Some countries had a lot of land, but little money. Many people were not allowed to worship as they wished. Several countries had large populations but weak armies. They all wanted what the others had, and they were willing to fight for it. The tension grew and grew. There was so much hatred, Europe felt like it was going to burst. Germany was one of the scariest countries. The government wanted to build the most powerful army in Europe to get rid of all of Germany's enemies.

When Albert arrived in 1913, Berlin was full of German soldiers that were trained, armed, and eager for war. It was a very uncomfortable place for the peace-loving

Albert to live. But one person in Berlin, Albert's cousin, Elsa, made life much more pleasant. Elsa was full of affection for Albert. They started to spend a lot of time together. Elsa was soon in love with Albert— the man, not the scientist. As far as Albert was concerned, he and Elsa were a much happier match than Albert and the challenging Mileva. Soon the couple announced that they were going to get married.

Elsa took care of Albert, which was good because

Albert certainly didn't. He was ever more careless about getting enough sleep and eating properly. Albert's doctor said of him, "As his mind knows no limits, so his body follows no set rules. He sleeps until he is wakened; he stays awake until he is told to go to bed; he will go hungry until he is given something to eat; and then, he eats until he is stopped." Elsa looked after him, making sure Albert got up on time, got dressed, and ate his breakfast.

Life with his second wife suited Albert very well. However, it is an interesting fact that Albert's very best scientific thinking was done during his marriage to Mileva. Perhaps that doesn't mean anything. Or perhaps, as some critics say, "his" great theories might really be "their" great theories? Or even "her" great theories? Some publications, even *Time* magazine (which proclaimed Albert Einstein "Person of the Century" in its December 31, 1999 issue) wondered exactly what Mileva may have contributed to her husband's scientific ideas.

An Einstein Thought

Albert claimed that space is curved. That's why a ray of light—instead of traveling forever in a straight line—might even return to where it started. Think about it. You're four years old and while you're out in the yard, you shine a flashlight into the sky. Ten years later, you're fourteen, mowing the lawn, and BLAM!—the same light smacks you in the eyes. Surprise!

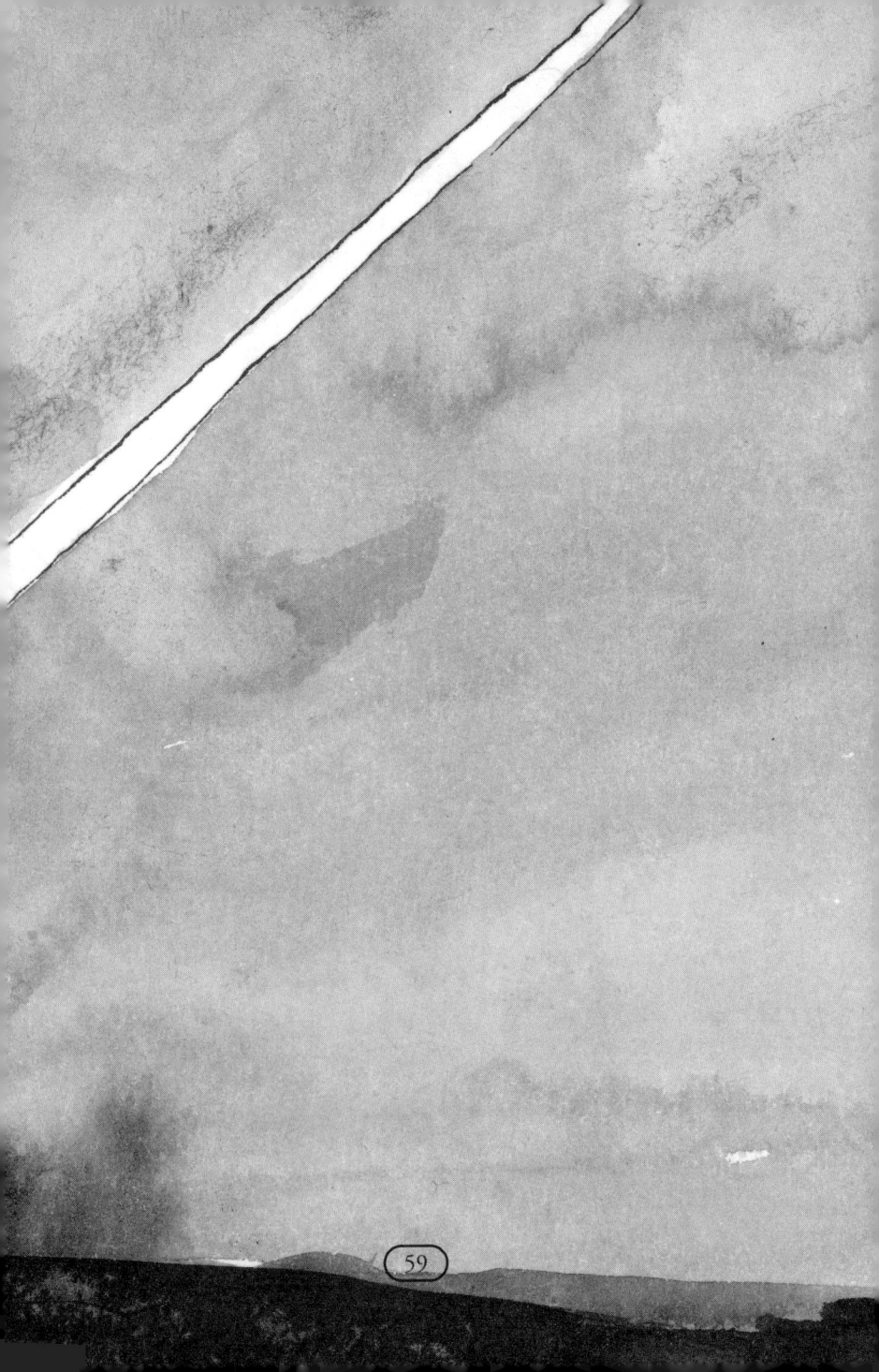

In 1914, Europe finally burst. The weak political agreements that had kept countries out of war
collapsed. World War I erupted, with Germany's
great armies facing France, Russia, and England,
and quickly winning many battles.

Wars run on hate, drain countries of food and money, and cause the deaths of many. Albert hated the war. He hated all wars. This war also brought a particular frustration to Albert. He had hoped to prove his theory of curving light through photos of the 1914 eclipse. Just as German scientists were setting up cameras in Russia, war broke out.

Germany and Russia were now enemies. The Russians arrested the German scientists and destroyed their equipment. The eclipse passed with no photos. It would be another five years before Albert would have a chance to photograph another total eclipse.

The combined forces of Russia, France, and England eventually slowed and stopped the German victories. The war became a stalemate. Year after year, neither side could gain clear victory over the other. The supplies needed to fight the long war drained Germany of its money, food, and fuel. And meanwhile, thousands of German soldiers died each day.

German leaders kept insisting that the war would end in their favor. They ordered the country's best scientists to say that, yes indeed, Germany was doing a great job fighting the war. Albert refused to make such a statement. He said, "Never do anything against conscience, even if the state demands it." And he meant it.

The German government was furious with Albert. It wanted to put Albert and his ridiculous head of hair into jail. But Albert was lucky. He was still a citizen of Switzerland. It was difficult for the Germans to imprison somebody from another country, especially a peaceful one like Switzerland.

Germany finally lost the war in 1918. Albert had managed to stay out of jail. More than ever, Albert was committed to promoting peace.

In the following year, 1919, there was going to be a full eclipse, the first since the one in 1914 that didn't get photographed. It was "step up or shut up" time for Albert and his theory of bending light. Many scientists in Germany hoped that Albert would be proven wrong. Then, perhaps, all his other theories would be ignored, too.

Before the eclipse, cameras were set up in two locations—one in South America and one on an island of the coast of West Africa. There were two cameras in case clouds suddenly moved in and blocked the eclipse in one place; that way, there was still a chance to get photos at the other location. The cameras were pointed at the sun. Ordinarily, the intense sunlight made it impossible to see or photograph the movement of light as it passed the sun and planets. But then the moon moved in between the sun and earth. It blocked the sun's brightness and suddenly light not seen before could be photographed. The cameras clicked.

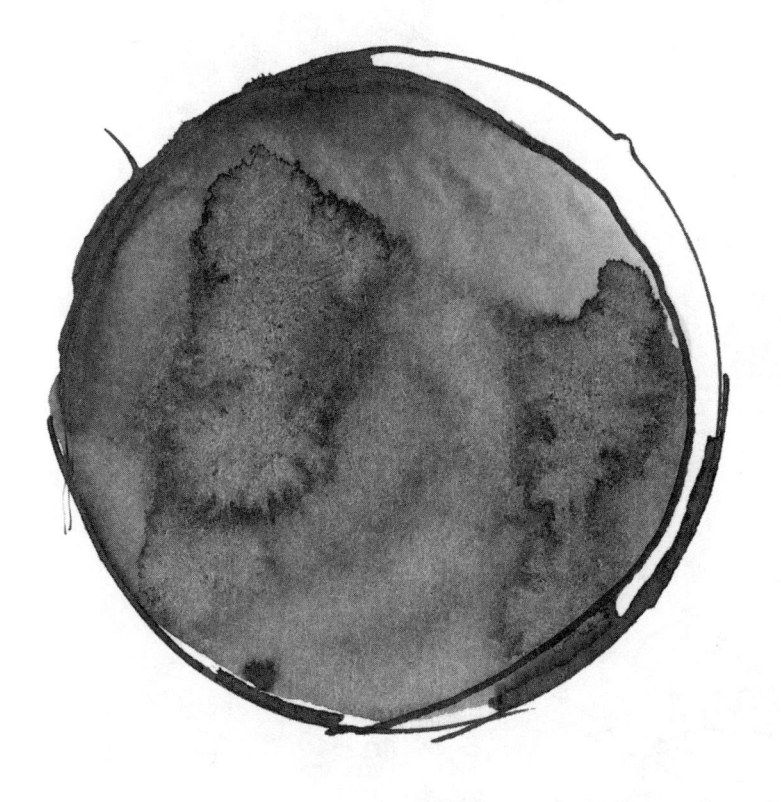

Once the photographs were developed, Albert was sure they would show that light bent as it passed the sun and other planets.

On November 7, 1919, the news was announced. Albert was right. Light did bend! Although very few people understood what Albert Einstein was talking about, the whole world

recognized that he was a genius. Suddenly, Albert was a superstar. A tobacco company even introduced a new product—"The Einstein Cigar." And within a year of the eclipse, over 100 books and articles about Albert were published. Now, eighty years later, the number of books and articles about Albert is in the thousands.

All the fuss may sound wonderful. But to Albert, it meant losing his treasured privacy. The attention, Albert wrote to a friend, was "so bad that I can hardly breathe, let alone get down to any sensible work." He was the first genius superstar.

Albert made the best of the uncomfortable situation. Because of his growing fame, he could have become rich by appearing on radio shows, making speeches, and writing books. A London theater offered Albert as much money as he wanted if Albert would appear on stage with fire-eaters and tightrope walkers. Albert's "act" would be explaining his theories. But Albert said no. Instead of making money, he wanted to use his influence to make the world a better place. For Albert, that meant a world without war.

Chapter 6
War . . . Again

"Unless the cause of peace based on law gathers behind it the force and zeal of a religion, it hardly can hope to succeed."

—Albert Einstein

Albert's fame brought him thousands of letters from people all over the world. Not just scientists, either—kids, newspaper reporters, political leaders, college students—they all wrote to him. Many of the letters came from Jewish people right in Germany. They were kept out of schools, denied jobs, and not allowed to vote. Albert was Jewish. Couldn't he do anything?

For a long time Albert wanted to help create a homeland for Jewish people. The current Jewish nation of Israel did not exist in the early 1900s.

The land where Israel is now was called Palestine. Like many other Jews, Albert thought that this area was where a Jewish homeland belonged. In 1921, Albert traveled with other important Jewish people to the United States. He wanted to raise money for a Jewish homeland in Palestine.

Albert enjoyed the long boat trip from Europe to America. He looked out at the endless ocean and felt "dissolved and immersed in nature." It reminded Albert how tiny one man was compared to the greatness of nature. He was not so important as the world was making him out to be. That thought, he said, "makes me happy."

N

JORDAN

PALESTINE

DEAD SEA

EGYPT

So Albert was quite surprised to see thousands of people, including reporters and photographers, waiting at the pier when his ship arrived in New York City. Wherever he went, there were huge crowds eager to see the genius who unlocked secrets of the universe. The mayor of New York personally welcomed him and presented Albert with a key to the city. There was a parade in his

honor. When Albert visited Washington, D.C., President Warren Harding invited him to the White House.

Albert's "eccentric genius look" was a big hit with Americans. With his wild hair, messy clothes, and friendly personality, Albert charmed reporters. He was often asked, "Could you briefly explain your theory of relativity?" This question drove Albert nuts. After all, it had taken him fifteen years of intense thinking to develop the theory. But he'd take a deep breath, smile, and say, "When a man sits with a pretty girl for an hour, it seems like a minute. But let him sit on a hot stove for a minute—and it's longer than any hour. That's relativity."

Although Albert was a superstar in the United

States, he was an unwanted problem in Germany. Although he still had his teaching job in Berlin, it became harder for Albert to stay in Germany with each passing year. After the Nazis took control of Germany in the 1920s, Albert's life was increasingly in danger. Nazis hated Jews, intellectuals, and pacifists. Albert was all three. When Nazis emptied university libraries of their books and burned them, it was often Albert's books that topped the huge bonfires.

By 1930, Albert had done most of his best scientific thinking. His focus now was on politics and public speaking. This made the Nazis even angrier. For his safety, Elsa pleaded with Albert to stop speaking out against the Nazis. He refused. He said, "I wouldn't be Einstein if I kept quiet." He also refused to leave Germany, even though more and more friends and family begged him to.

The Einsteins did, however, take many trips to more welcoming countries. They traveled to the

Middle East, to Asia, and to the west coast of the United States. Everywhere they went, they were greeted by large, cheering crowds. Japan even declared the day of Albert's arrival there a national holiday. In Spain, he was greeted by the king and thousands of fans.

Albert received honorary degrees from Oxford, Cambridge, the Sorbonne, Harvard, and many other universities around the world. He was a guest professor, raised funds for Jewish causes, and warned of the growing political hatred in Germany. How strange for Albert to be adored all over the world except in the country where he had been born. The Nazis published a book called "One Hundred Authors Against Einstein." All Albert said was, "Why one hundred? If I were wrong, one would have been enough."

Hitler and the Nazis

Germany could not recover from their defeat in World War I. The treaty that ended the war left Germans hungry, poor, and feeling hopeless. The Nazis (National Socialist Party) blamed Germany's problems on people of the Jewish religion. By the early 1930's, the Nazi party had grown from a small band of people with extremely dangerous ideas to the most

powerful political party in Germany. The Nazis were led by Adolf Hitler, who became Chancellor of Germany in 1933. Hitler's government denied Jews a normal life. They could not go to school, hold jobs, own property, or worship. Eventually, the Nazis began murdering the Jews. They wanted to wipe every Jew off the face of the earth. The Nazis killed six million Jews before World War II ended in 1945 and Germany was defeated.

Albert was very lucky to have survived in Nazi Germany. In 1931, while Albert was a guest professor in California, Adolf Hitler declared Albert a spy. Hitler put out a death warrant for Albert. In 1933, while Albert and Elsa were returning home from their trip to California, Nazis broke into the Einsteins' summer house in Caputh, Germany. A bread knife was found in the kitchen—a perfectly natural place for a bread knife to be. But the Nazis 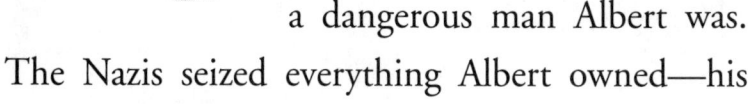 used the knife as "proof" of what a dangerous man Albert was. The Nazis seized everything Albert owned—his home and his money.

Now there was no question about moving. Albert and Elsa rented a house in Belgium where Albert's stepdaughters also came to live. But in Belgium, a new book from Germany was now available. It included photographs of Nazi enemies. Albert's photo was on the very first page with the

words "not yet hanged" printed next to it. Belgium was not a safe place to stay either. But where would the Einsteins go? England? No. Elsa was afraid to live there. In England, the Nazis had offered a huge reward for Albert's murder. Albert joked, "I never knew that I was worth so much." In the end, Albert and Elsa decided that the United States would be their new home.

NOT YET HANGED

Albert became a professor of mathematics at the Institute for Advance Study in Princeton, New Jersey. (Albert asked for a salary of $3,000. Elsa got that upped to $16,000.) By the end of 1933, he and Elsa had settled into the small college town.

The early years in Princeton were very difficult. Albert was 54 years old. He was not a young man. He was no longer startling the world with new ideas. Then, just three years after their move to Princeton, Elsa passed away. Albert was lonely and heartbroken. His own health suffered. He had

barely left Elsa's side for the last twelve months of her life. Albert also kept hearing about friends who had been murdered in Germany.

With all of the energy that he had left, he was determined to do whatever he could to stop the Nazis. He played the violin at fund-raising concerts. But that was not going to put an end to Hitler.

Albert's famous equation, $E = mc^2$, said that if just a few atoms were converted to energy, the amount of energy produced would be massive. In 1939, Albert learned that European scientists were at work trying to make an atomic bomb. Albert feared what the Germans would do if they were the first to build such a bomb. So Albert wrote a letter to the President of the United States, Franklin D. Roosevelt. He asked that the United States begin developing an atomic bomb right away.

This could not have been an easy letter for a man like Albert to write. He hated war. He hated weapons. Yet now he was asking the United States to hurry up and build the most destructive bomb ever imagined. Even the simplest atomic bomb could destroy an entire city and kill thousands of people within seconds. But Albert thought that it would be worse if the Nazis were the only ones with such a weapon. Partly because of Albert's letter, President Roosevelt had secret work begun on building an atomic bomb.

The Atomic Bomb

In World War II, Japan joined forces with Germany and Italy. So now there were two fronts, or areas of battle— Europe and the islands in the Pacific Ocean. In late 1941, the United States joined the countries (England, France) in the fight against Germany and Japan. American troops were sent to both battlefronts.

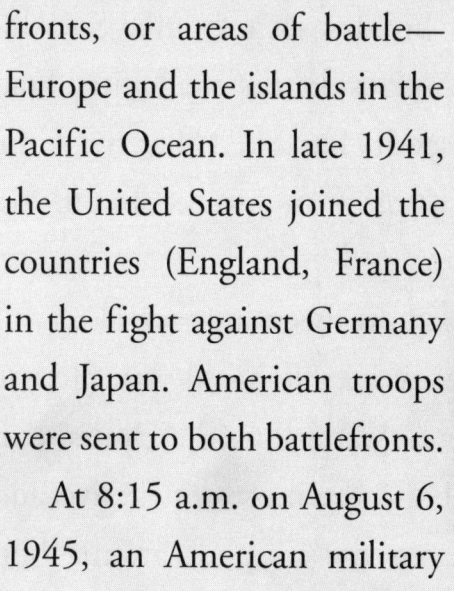

At 8:15 a.m. on August 6, 1945, an American military plane released an atomic bomb over the Japanese city of Hiroshima. In an instant, 80,000 people were killed. Hiroshima simply ceased to exist. People at the blast's center

were vaporized. All that remained was their charred shadows on the walls of buildings.

Three days later, the U.S. dropped another bomb on another Japanese city, Nagasaki.

Japan soon surrendered, and World War II finally came to an end.

The world now had weapons that were destructive beyond imagination. Decades of scientific thought and research, including Einstein's, made the atomic bomb a possibility. War made it a reality. The world was never the same again.

HIROSHIMA

NAGASAKI

Albert later reflected on this moment in world history. "I made one great mistake in my life—when I signed the letter to President Roosevelt recommending that atom bombs be made . . . but there was some justification—the danger that the Germans would make them."

After World War II, Albert spent time and energy trying to limit the development of atomic weapons. "I do not know how the third world war will be fought," he warned, "but I do know how the fourth will: with sticks and stones." What he meant was that after a third world war with atomic bombs, the modern world would be destroyed and humans would have to go back to living like cavemen. "We scientists," Albert said, "must consider it our solemn duty to do all in our power in preventing these weapons from being used."

Even today some people blame Einstein for the atom bomb because he discovered the relationship between mass and energy. But can anybody blame

Isaac Newton—who first explained the laws of gravity—for every plane that crashes to the ground?

In 1940, at age 61, Albert became a citizen of the United States. For the rest of his life he remained in Princeton, New Jersey, and worked on something called "The Unified Field Theory." But, surprisingly, Albert never produced a finished theory.

In many ways, Albert's life had come full circle. Toward the end of his life he wrote, "I am generally regarded as a sort of petrified object, rendered deaf and blind by the years." He loved to take walks, just as he always had. And although Albert never drove a car, he loved to sail. He would take out a one-engine boat, aim it at other boats, and then—at the last moment—swerve aside.

In Princeton, he was a familiar sight, walking back and forth between his home and office, often chatting with neighbors. (He spoke English with an accent. "I tink I will a little study." "She is a very good theory.") His shaggy hair, now white, grew even wilder and he often went without socks, belt, or suspenders. Once some boys asked Albert why he never wore socks. With a sly smile he answered that he was now old enough that if he didn't want to, he didn't have to.

On his walks, Albert was known to stop and help a child fix a bicycle. And when a young girl came to his house asking for help with her

math homework, Albert not only did just that, but shared his lunch of a can of baked beans with her.

As for his own children, Albert rarely saw his sons. Hans Albert had fled Nazi Germany and later moved to California; Eduard and Mileva remained safe in Switzerland where Mileva died in 1948.

Albert's sister and best friend, Maja, came to live with him in Princeton. As a child, Albert had a horrible temper that once led him to hit Maja in the head. In these later years, she'd smile and say, "To be the sister of a thinker, you must have a very thick skull."

Life in Princeton was pleasant. In the evenings, just as Albert and his mother used to play duets, he played violin with other musicians. He ended up spending the last twenty years of his life at his

house at 112 Mercer Street in Princeton. He loved the old house, its gardens, and the way the light came through the windows. When they first moved to Mercer Street, Elsa had a picture window put in Albert's study. From there, Albert could enjoy the beauty and mystery of nature as he always had, watching birds fly, flowers bloom, and the morning sunrise.

Chapter 7
Albert's Time Is Up

"Everything is determined, the beginning as well as the end, by forces over which we have no control. It is determined for the insect as well as for the star. Human beings, vegetables or cosmic dust, we all dance to a mysterious tune, intoned in the distance by an invisible player."

—Albert Einstein

By 1948, Albert was in very poor health. His heart was getting weaker and weaker. A doctor insisted that Albert take a certain medicine. Albert hesitated. The doctor insisted. So Albert took the medicine and immediately got sick to his stomach. "There," he snapped at the doctor, "do you feel better now?"

Yet there was reason for happiness during those

years. In 1948 the Jewish nation of Israel was created. Albert was overjoyed. All his work had helped to bring about something wonderful. After Israel's first president died, Albert was asked to become the next president. Albert said no. "Politics is for the moment," he once wrote, "while an equation is for eternity." Still he was greatly honored by the offer.

In 1950, Albert made his will. He wanted all his science papers left to the Hebrew University in Jerusalem. In 1951, Maja died. Now Albert had neither his wife nor sister. He was more alone than ever. He surrounded himself with family photographs. He said, "A photograph never grows old. You and I change, people change all through the months and years but a photograph always remains the same. How nice to look at a photograph of a mother or father taken many years ago. You see them as you remember them. That is why I think a photograph can be kind."

Several years later, after a brief illness, Albert was admitted to the Princeton hospital. On April 17, 1955, he asked that his eyeglasses, some paper, and a pen be brought to his hospital bed. He had work—thinking—to do. The next day he died with a sheet of equations next to him. To the very end Albert was thinking. The last letter he wrote was one that urged all nations to give up nuclear weapons.

The Einstein house at 112 Mercer Street in Princeton, New Jersey, is treated no differently than any other home in the neighborhood. That's the way Albert wanted it. He worried that if it was turned into a museum, people would concern themselves too much with his memory and not enough with their own future.

After Albert's death, the scientific community mourned the loss of a great and original mind.

Jews mourned the loss of a leader who always wished for a better and more peaceful world, even in the darkest moments of Jewish history.

And all people mourned the loss of a unique, peace-loving man. Perhaps Albert said it best, "Only a life lived for others is a life worthwhile."

Albert was not the best husband. He was not the best father. But as a friend said of Albert, he was "the freest man I have known."

Chapter 8
A Final Thought

Albert left these instructions upon his death: donate my brain to science, cremate my body, and throw the ashes in some secret place.

This was done.

So where is Albert's brain now?

After Albert died, an autopsy was done on his

 body. In the process, the doctor, Thomas Harvey removed Albert's brain, studied it, decided that there was nothing all that special about it, and set it aside in a bottle of formaldehyde.

Later, when Dr. Harvey moved to Wichita, Kansas, he took the brain with him. He kept the brain, which was in pieces, in two jars inside a cardboard box labeled "Cider." Since then, further studies by several medical researchers have found Albert's brain to be a bit more interesting than Dr. Harvey did. (Dr. Harvey provided the researchers with pieces of the brain.) Albert's brain weighed less than the average brain, was 15 percent wider, and had an unusual set of grooves. Yet the importance of these differences remains unknown.

Harvey kept the brain with him for over forty years.

One time, Harvey and Michael Paterniti, an author, put the brain in the trunk of a car and drove it all the way to California so that a piece of it could be given to Albert's granddaughter, Evelyn. Soon after that trip, Harvey turned the brain over to a Princeton hospital where it continues to float around in a jar.

You have to wonder what Albert would think of that!

Albert Einstein
1879–1955

Timeline of Albert's Life

1879	Albert is born, March 14, in Germany
1881	Albert's sister Maja is born
1889	Albert starts high school
1894	Albert's family moves to Italy, leaving him in school in Germany
1899	Albert decides to become a Swiss citizen
1900	Albert graduates from college
1902	Albert gets a job at the Patent Office
1903	Albert marries Mileva Maric
1905	Albert introduces his theory of relativity
1909	Albert becomes a professor at the University of Zurich
1914	Albert leaves Mileva and his sons and move to Berlin, Germany Albert must wait to prove his theory of curving light
1919	Albert marries Elsa
1921	Albert visits the United States
1922	Albert wins the Nobel Prize for Physics
1931	Albert is declared a spy; Hitler puts out a death warrant for him
1933	Albert and Elsa move to Princeton, New Jersey
1936	Death of Elsa
1940	Albert becomes a U.S. citizen
1948	Death of Mileva
1951	Albert's sister Maja dies
1955	Albert dies on April 18

TIMELINE OF THE WORLD

Thomas Edison invents the lightbulb	1879
Clara Barton founds the American Red Cross	1881
The Eiffel Tower is completed in Paris Vincent van Gogh paints *The Starry Night*	1889
X-rays are discovered (1895) The first movie is shown in Paris (1895)	1894
The first modern Olympics are held in Greece (1896)	1899
Dr. Sigmund Freud publishes *The Interpretation of Dreams*	1900
The first *Tyrannosaurus rex* fossil is discovered	1902
The Wright brothers fly the first plane	1903
The first movie theater opens	1905
American Robert Peary reaches the North Pole	1909
The Titanic sinks (1912) The first crossword puzzle appears in a New York newspaper (1913) Outbreak of World War I	1914
World War I ends (1918)	1919
The first highway opens in Germany	1921
King Tut's tomb is found	1922
"The Star-Spangled Banner" becomes the U.S. national anthem	1931
Adolf Hitler becomes Chancellor of Germany	1933
Franklin D. Roosevelt is re-elected president The game *Monopoly* is invented	1936
Outbreak of World War II (1939)	1940
World War II ends (1945) FDR dies and Harry Truman becomes president (1945) The nation of Israel is created	1948
The phrase "rock and roll" is used on the radio for the first time *I Love Lucy* premieres on TV	1951
Disneyland opens in California	1955